Lovest Thou Me More Than These:

Heaven's Question For Our Times

David Israel

The Key of David Press

Atlanta, Georgia

Published in 2023 by The Key of David Press, LLC

Library of Congress Cataloging-in-Publication Data:
An application to register this book for cataloging has been submitted to the Library of Congress.
International Standard Book Number: 979-8-9878482-0-3

Bible quotations are usually from the King James Version unless otherwise noted, with Hebrew names substituted for the Greco-Roman words God, Lord, Jesus, Holy Spirit, et al.

Printed in the United States of America.

Table of Contents

Introduction

Photography coursed through my veins and flowed through my lineage. My grandfather had become the first Black photographer in a mid-sized city in the deep South before the Civil Rights era. I grew up as a little boy running behind Granddad at his studio. I sipped from his endless supply of Coca Colas with which he plied me, and learned how to develop film and negatives. I watched how he posed people for the camera.

The business he built, photographing both white and Black weddings, schools, couples, and other events, supported his family for decades. His sons, my father and uncle, each inherited his affection for the camera. My brother has also loaded up on pricey cameras.

My daughter also has taken to the camera, becoming not only the unofficial family photographer, but also the unofficial photographer for school functions and family events.

But me? I've got more of an amateur's thirst than a knack for it. Still, that didn't stop me from pulling out my little camera phone and shooting thousands and thousands of pictures over the years. One day, Most High willing, I look forward to sharing my story of driving thirteen thousand miles from coast to coast throughout the United States. I traveled to every state, and almost every high place, in the continental U.S. I went to the Father in each one, asking Him to do His perfect will in all those places. The things I saw, the people I met, the voice of YAHUAH blanketing me in a soaring wind the Grand Canyon…

But all that's for another day.

Today, I return to the night in January 2023 when I went looking for a place to dump trash. A couple of boxes rode with me almost like passengers in my car, and needed a new home in someone's dumpster. I didn't want to wait another week for trash pickup, so I decided to take matters into my own hands.

Near my home, an older mall with only one or two tenants sat mostly vacant. So, when I saw the parking lot full of eighteen-wheeler trucks one night, it raised my eyebrows. Some of the semi-trucks bore the logos of logistics companies, some of which I had never seen before. The mall's sole remaining major tenant, a movie theater, had predictably drawn a large retinue of movie fans. Curiosity seduced me, so I drove slowly past the pile of cars and headed to the back of the mall to see what I could see.

What I saw shocked me. After passing a Covid testing and vaccination tent on the mall's side, I paused. As I drove in an unhurried manner, I saw lines of cars, including one lurking silently at the back of the lot far from the mall's façade. Its headlights sat on, puncturing the otherwise shallow darkness that enveloped the area.

But as I continued looking, I saw large light poles, brightly lit. More brightly lit than most active malls. The area carried all the tell-tale signs of a construction zone.

Except there were no signs. Typically, the construction contractors want to advertise that they are managing a project, or partnering with another vendor in a joint-bid to operate the construction project. But not here. No signage. No clue as to what was being built. Nothing.

From my untrained eyes, I even saw what looked like the beginnings of an electrical transformer, or a utility substation. I had not expected this. You couldn't see even a hint of this from any of the roadways that surrounded the mall. From a driver casually passing by, it was simply another dying mall mostly shrouded in darkness.

But I was shocked. And that shock flashed through me to activate a primal impulse that frequently hit me: "grab the camera!" my body shrieked silently.

I whipped it out like a skilled samurai (at least in my mind) and began shooting pictures of the buildings, the cars, the overflowing dumpsters. I continued my snail-paced drive in shock. What were ALL these cars doing here after ten pm at night, working in so much darkness? There were so many of them, that I had a deep gut-level impression, one that I could neither shake nor account for, that there was a massive project being developed deep ***underground***.

Whoever had hired this construction crew had to be paying these workers time and a half, at least. Even more, the mall was nearly deserted. Multiple development plans had been floated before the community, yet none of them had ever materialized in the six years since the property's anchor tenant vacated.

But here I sat, watching what appeared to be a mighty construction project, mostly unseen, totally unadvertised, and possibly underground. And a project without a shred of newspaper coverage or commentary.

I thought about dumping my trash boxes, but the Ruach ha Qodesh told me that it would not be wise, not with the cameras visible everywhere, not with whatever was happening.

After shooting many pictures and eyeing several overflowing trash dumpsters, I felt a piercing drive to get out of there. Quickly! Turning my car around, I began heading toward the exit.

Only, it wasn't an exit anymore. Whoever was redeveloping the mall had put up cones and blocked the lanes so you had to enter and exit in very particular ways. So I turned around. But not before I saw a security guard vehicle slowly moving in my general direction.

I prayed that it was heading around the mall in another direction. But the Father didn't answer that exact prayer, because the security guard had started heading right. Toward. Me.

Yes, I had been shooting pictures like crazy. Yes, I had been praying out loud as I drove. But had I aroused that much suspicion?

Apparently, I had.

A slow sense of panic began welling up inside of me, and I turned the corner and began zooming back to reverse my previous path around the mall. I wanted to hit the gas like a professional racer and streak out as fast as my little car would go. Except there he was: another security guard, just sitting in front of the mall, directly in my lane of traffic.

I hurried past him as quickly as I could while still trying to appear casual. Peering into his car window as I rolled past him, I saw him leaning casually away, talking into his radio microphone. And looking right at me.

Whatever he was saying, I put my foot on the accelerator to rush past him. I rode past the vaccination tent. I passed the large cluster of movie afficionados at the front of the mall, then left out of the parking lot and into the city street as quickly as I could go.

I looked over my shoulder for any sign that a guard had tailed me, but I saw no one. That didn't keep me from continuing to look over the next few miles. No one could tell me I wasn't evading detection like Jason Bourne.

Eventually, I dropped off my trash at a different destination, and made it back home safely. Thankfully, no one sat in a darkened vehicle at the end of the cul-de-sac watching me as I pulled into my garage.

Still, the whole episode taught me a lesson. My curiosity wrestled me into a possibly unwise course. My love of photography and chronicling things could have led me into a bad place if I had stubbornly stuck around. I needed to be thoughtful and strategic about what I did, rather than impetuous and impulsive.

I needed a framework and guide to order my steps and lead me correctly. Sometimes, the Most High has spoken to me most powerfully not through thunderous declarations, but through still, small questions.

As a young member of a famous televangelist's megachurch, I was enamored with the preacher's charisma. But the Father asked me a very quiet but probing question: 'Does this man preach like my servant Paul?' That simple question slapped me out of the spell in which the preacher's words bound me. Answering that drove me into a completely new direction in my quest for the Father.

In the same way, ABBA YAHUAH has a question that can help each of us wrestle with where we truly are with Him, not just where we think we SHOULD be. Only the Father can x-ray our souls to help us examine ourselves. This can help us determine how He truly feels about us, whether we really are right with Him and even in the faith. Or whether we're just modern day versions of the rich young ruler, deluding ourselves with our own pretense of righteousness.

So, exactly what is the question that operates like Heaven's spiritual x-ray of our lives? Let's find out together.

Chapter 1, YAHUAH's Glory

"The voice of YAHUAH maketh the hinds to calve, and discovereth the forests: and in his temple doth every one speak of his glory."

-Psalm 29:9

Checkmate. That's what the anointed cherub, who had once covered the throne of the Most High YAH, heard and saw in trembling anguish. The fallen one, gorgeous and brilliant, wily and wicked, had spoken and entranced millions and millions of exalted beings. He had seduced a third of Heaven's host in a rebellion against the King of Heaven. He had gleefully defiled the very courts of Heaven itself. He had enchanted the very sons of ELOHIYM into mutiny against their Father, curdling their hearts into permanent, twisted throes of hatred and envy.

With so many millions at his beck and call, and with his hegemony over the planet complete and secure, he thought he had won. It was just a matter of time....

Satan imagined he had figured out YAHUAH, and had developed a fool-proof plan to take down the Eternal Deity. But as he has painfully learned, no mistake is easier to make than to assume the Most High YAHUAH thinks like we do. Most of the people who even bother to read the Bible fool themselves into thinking that His Word is what we want to hear, and about what we want it to be about. We could imagine that our preoccupations are what keeps the Most High God up at night.

We could easily assume that. But we would be totally wrong. Isaiah 55:8 tells us His thoughts are not our thoughts, nor are our ways His ways.

Marching forward in our desire to make the Most High like us could seduce us to think the Bible is about us and what we want, our felt needs, our appetites and desires. But each of those thoughts would be wrong.

The Bible is YAHUAH's Hebrew book about His chosen people, a nation He called to manifest His glory and majesty in the midst of a world in open revolt against Him.

When did the world revolt against the Most High? All history shows it.

The World's Revolt Against YAHUAH

Adam and Eve disobeyed YAHUAH's commandments in the Garden of Eden. When they did that, they transformed themselves from conduits of the Most High's light and became pipes of darkness. They re-established themselves in the world as monuments of disobedience. That disobedience is what they bequeathed to their offspring.

The first parents' sin ripened into their son Cain's murder of their other son, Abel. Adam and Eve grieved in losing their beloved child. But they also ached with sorrow at the bitterness of knowing their own sin had corrupted Cain and ripened into his murder.

This sin did not end with Cain's ungodliness and rebellion. The rebellion filled the hearts of all men. It made them servants to Satan and the innumerable host of fallen angels, demons and monsters over which he ruled as king.

Eventually, the disobedience caused all the world to reverence Satan, his fallen angels, and their evil children, the Nephilim. Men's religion was evil through and through. But it wasn't just men's worship that was evil, but also their works. Every thought that passed through men's minds was divorced from YAHUAH. Humanity did not consider Him in their ways, and became foolish.

In anger, YAHUAH ELOHIYM destroyed the entire planet with a great flood. He saved only Noah and his seven relatives. Making a new covenant through faithful Noah, the Most High started the whole world over again.

But Satan, the anointed cherub who had once covered YAHUAH's throne and led Heaven's worship, would not stop his opposition to the Most High. Satan's own sin cost him his exalted position. In return, he wanted to take YAHUAH's place as ruler of creation.

First, Satan tried but failed to seduce the Most High into betraying His own righteousness and mercy by killing disobedient Adam after eating the forbidden fruit.

Next, the devil again used the same principle to try to force YAHUAH to break His fidelity to His own glory. He did this by creating the Nephilim, a hybrid human-angelic race that openly tyrannized humanity. Satan thought all the world would be defiled and then destroyed. He did not reckon on YAHUAH's mercy to a remnant in preserving eight people from the judgment of the Flood.

Nimrod, Satan's Plan of Judgment

Satan next tried to oppress humanity and oppose the Most High by creating a tyrannical god-man king named Nimrod. But once again, YAHUAH frustrated Satan by raising up a new remnant right in Nimrod's face. The Most High raised up a man named Abraham right out of Nimrod's city of Ur of the Chaldeans.

The Judgment of Egypt, Satan's Seat

In fury, after Nimrod's death, Satan fixed his capital in a new place: Egypt. Also known as Mizraim, the children of Egypt worshiped hundreds of gods, including Amen-Ra, Osiris, Isis, Set and Anubis. The kings of Egypt were Nephilim, demonstrated through their elongated heads as evidenced by their royal headgear and sometimes even their gigantic size. Many works, written by both contemporary and later historians, show the Pharaohs' powers, including supernatural strength and occult knowledge.

All of them, however, served the cobra snake, symbolizing Satan. Egypt became the epicenter of the devil's power and presence in the world.

But ABBA YAHUAH outsmarted Satan once more. He engineered circumstances so as to lead Joseph, Abraham's great grandson, into Egypt. The Father raised Joseph up from slavery and imprisonment to become the second in command to Pharaoh, where the son of Jacob helped the Egyptian empire prepare for an upcoming worldwide famine.

As famine stalked all the countries of the world, Joseph brought his father Jacob, and his brothers and their families, into Egypt for food and protection. The Book of Genesis describes how YAHUAH's chosen people descended into the devil's earthly headquarters.

The children of Israel fled the famine in Canaan. Under Joseph's rule, they stayed in Mizraim, becoming a mighty nation of millions.

The Israelites' growth and prosperity alarmed Pharaoh. Satan filled his heart and reduced all the children of Israel to slavery. As slaves, they built Pharaoh's cities, harvested his crops, and generated immense wealth for the empire.

Once more, as the Israelites toiled in slavery, it appeared that the devil had taken the upper hand against YAH and His people. Hillel (the devil's true name) even inspired Pharaoh to kill the firstborn males in an effort to destroy the Seed prophesied in Genesis 3.

The Call of Moses

Satan's plot to destroy the promised deliverer failed. Moses, the youngest son of Amnon and Jochebed, answered YAHUAH's call. Although an Israelite, he grew up in Pharaoh's court, raised as grandson to Pharaoh and in line to rule the world's greatest empire. He spent the first four decades of his life as an Egyptian prince.

But even though Moses sensed he had been chosen by YAHUAH to deliver his brothers, he trusted in himself. In anger, he killed an Egyptian taskmaster. In response, his uncle the Pharaoh issued an arrest warrant for Moses, and sought to kill him. Moses fled and became a shepherd in Midian, where he raised a family and a herd of sheep for forty years.

During Moses' forty years of exile, ABBA YAHUAH had prepared Moses, refining his character. In the anonymity of tending sheep on the backside of the desert for decades, Moses became as meek as he had once been impetuous and arrogant. Numbers 12:3 tells us, "***Now the man Moses was very meek, above all the men which were upon the face of the earth.***"

The Most High chose Moses for the mission of delivering His chosen people from slavery. Moses' humility made him the most suitable instrument for the Father's use. ABBA communed with Moses, and inhabited him. YAHUAH refuses to dwell with, in, or around those who are not humble as Moses was humble.

Moses returned from Midian back into Egypt after a century of Israel's bondage. Working with his brother Aaron and in submission to the guidance of the Father, they delivered ten devastating plagues that crippled Egypt's food supply, water supply, and economy.

Pharaoh continued his refusal to release Israel until YAHUAH killed the Egyptians' firstborn children.

In joy in the midst of the Egyptians' heartbreak, the children of Israel departed Egypt on the night of the first Passover. But even after freeing the Israelites, Pharaoh cleaved to his rage against Israel. He took his army and pursued them to the Red Sea. There, they met their final judgment from YAHUAH.

First, Moses lifted up his arms and divided the sea for the Israelites to cross. When the Egyptians pursued them, the land which had been dry turned muddy, and the Egyptians soldiers and charioteers began dying by the thousands.

In horror, the Egyptian army began to retreat. But Moses then stretched out his hands and brought the walls of the sea back down, crushing and drowning the remaining Egyptians. Even Pharaoh perished in the waves of the Red Sea.

The Marriage Between YAHUAH and His People

Three months later, YAHUAH led the Israelite camp to Mount Sinai. This was the mountaintop where the Most High first commissioned Moses to become a shepherd to His people. At Mount Sinai, YAHUAH entered into a marital covenant with the children of Israel as His bride. These were the marital vows YAH made with Israel:

> 4 Ye have seen what I did unto the Egyptians, and how I bare you on eagles' wings, and brought you unto myself.
>
> 5 Now therefore, if ye will obey my voice indeed, and keep my covenant, then ye shall be a peculiar treasure unto me above all people: for all the earth is mine:
>
> 6 And ye shall be unto me a kingdom of priests, and an holy nation. These are the words which thou shalt speak unto the children of Israel.[1]

On that day, the children of Israel became the special, covenant people of the Creator God YAHUAH. In unison, all the Israelites promised Him, "***All that YAHUAH hath spoken we will do.***"[2]

Through His servant Moses, YAH promised freedom and greatness, and began to teach them His laws, statutes, and commandments. He also commanded them to build a Tabernacle.

The Tabernacle

The Tabernacle was intended to be the center of worship for the people. It was the brain child of Moses' experience with YAHUAH in Mount Sinai. For forty days and forty nights, Moses met with and talked with the Most High, Who had descended in fire upon the mountaintop.

Moses received the Ten Commandments, but he also received far more. He received all of the Father's statutes. He also saw the entire early history of the world, from the creation to Adam and Eve, all the way down to the lives of Abraham and his descendants through Jacob and his sons. YAH inspired Moses to write it all.

But there was another feature of Moses' time on the Mount that we don't think about enough. It was the fact that he spent time in YAHUAH's presence. The Father brought heaven down to Mount Sinai. Not Heaven in some generalized way, but the very throne room of Heaven.

This is how Moses saw the original Tabernacle of YAHUAH in Heaven. It awed and inspired the prophet. He saw the worship of the angels, archangels, and cherubim. Moses himself wanted to bring to earth what he saw in heaven.

This is why we read, in Exodus 25:9, YAHUAH tells Moses, "***According to all that I shew thee, after the pattern of the tabernacle, and the pattern of all the instruments thereof, even so shall ye make it.***" ABBA showed Moses the Tabernacle of Heaven so Moses could duplicate that Tabernacle on earth.

We read this again, in the Father's direction to Moses in Exodus 25:40: "***And look that thou make them after their pattern, which was shewed thee in the mount.***"

Everything for Moses was about duplicating the life of Heaven here on Earth. We see this in two ways.

First, YAHUAH delivered His laws, or Torah, to Israel so that they could walk in ABBA's ways. This holiness would allow the Most High to dwell among the people. After all, Revelation 21:27 warns, "***And there shall in no wise enter into it* ANYTHING THAT DEFILETH, *neither whatsoever worketh abomination, or maketh a lie: but they which are written in the Lamb's book of life***" (emphasis added). No defiled person can stand in YAH's presence.

But the second way is crucially important as well: not only must the people be perfect, but the worship must be perfect. The worship involves the Tabernacle, the offerings, the incense, the prayer and praise of YAHUAH. The Tabernacle that Moses and the Israelites created mirrored what Moses had seen in heaven.

The Lengths of Time

The Bible is very careful to describe timelines for Israel's marriage to YAHUAH, and the construction of the Tabernacle. In Exodus 19:1, we read, "***In the third month, when the children of Israel were gone forth out of the land of Egypt, the same day came they into the wilderness of Sinai.***"

When the Scriptures say this was the third month, it meant that they had been freed from Egyptian bondage for around ninety days. Three months. This is very important, because three is a number in Scripture which often carries prophetic meaning. It appears four hundred and sixty-seven times in the Bible, and connotes harmony, perfection, completeness, and newness of life.

In Hebrew thought, three symbolized the intensity of completeness. It is why the holy angels of Isaiah 6 cry out, "Holy! Holy! Holy!" back and forth to one another when praising YAHUAH. They were rejoicing in and extolling the total and complete set-apartness of YAHUAH from creation.

We see three used, for instance, when YAHUSHA told His disciple Peter to feed His sheep three times. When YAHUAH called Samuel in the Tabernacle, He called the boy three times. We also see that the fathers of Israel were Abraham, Isaac, and Jacob, or three men.

And while some dispute the concept of the Trinity as a Christian invention, this accusation would have surprised King David. As with many of the other prophets, David often spoke directly to the second member of the Trinity, Adonai YAHUAH, instead of the Father. Also, in Psalm 51:11, David pleaded with the Father to not take away from him the Father's Ruach ha Qodesh, or Holy Spirit.

The three-fold nature of YAHUAH as Father, Son and Spirit is reflected in the very fabric and warp of the Hebraic thinking of our forefathers. While outside the scope of this book to dive deep into the subject, we can see this truth most vividly when we consider YAHUAH's revelation that He, in His essence, is fire. Both Deuteronomy 4:24 and Hebrews 12:29 tell us that YAH is fire. The living and eternal communication between the Father and the Son consists of the wind, or breath, or Spirit, of the First and Second Persons of the Trinity. So just as YAHUAH the Father and YAHUAH the Son are eternal, so is Their mind, YAHUAH the Ruach, or Set Apart Spirit.

This explains why we can only know spiritual truth concerning the Father as it is revealed to us by the Son through the Ruach. The Apostle Paul confirms this in 1 Corinthians 2:9-16. The Messiah Himself teaches this truth in John 3:1-13, and again in John 16:13-14, where He states:

> 13 Howbeit when he, the Ruach of truth, is come, he will guide you into all truth: for he shall not speak of himself; but whatsoever he shall hear, that shall he speak: and he will shew you things to come.
>
> 14 He shall glorify me: for he shall receive of mine, and shall shew it unto you.

YAHUSHA clearly teaches here that it is the Set Apart Spirit who will guide YAHUSHA's disciples into all truth. How does the Spirit do this? By taking from the heart of the Second Person of the Trinity, and from the Father, to show deep spiritual things to those who belong to YAHUAH through YAHUSHA.

The fact that the children of Israel had been delivered for three months when YAHUAH entered into the sacred marital covenant is crucially important. This fact points to the total shalom, wholeness, and harmony for which YAHUAH had called Abraham, Isaac, and Jacob. The Heavenly Father intended the offspring of those men to be the holy seed who would transform the planet through their worship and their set apart life.

The children of Israel's meeting and marriage with YAHUAH in the wilderness at Mount Sinai in the third month reflected the Father's total harmony, or shalom. Israel entered into a completely new life, an experience not shared by any other nation on earth.

But this holy covenant of divine marriage was only the beginning. After the marriage ceremony of Exodus 19, YAHUAH commissioned the construction of the Tabernacle. We won't go into details, as those are explained at length in Exodus 25 – 40. But what we will look at is how long it took to build the Tabernacle. That time line is extremely important. It conveys critical truths for those who want a more intimate relationship with YAHUAH.

So, exactly how long did it take to complete the Tabernacle? In Exodus 40:2, YAHUAH commanded, "***On the first day of the first month shalt thou set up the tabernacle of the tent of the congregation.***" This meant that exactly one year after Israel departed Israel, they would complete and rear up the tent of meeting.

So, let's think about it. It took three months after leaving Egypt for YAHUAH to let the stain of Egyptian life, culture, and worship work themselves out of the Israelites' systems. Three months before they were sanctified in His eyes, and could devote themselves to YAHUAH in an everlasting covenant. And then, twelve months after leaving Egypt, they had completed the Tabernacle. So exactly how long did it take to build?

The process of completing the Tabernacle, started in the third month and concluded on the first day of the next year. Exodus 40:17 confirms it: "*And it came to pass in the first month in the second year, on the first day of the month, that the tabernacle was reared up.*"

That means that the length of time to build the Tabernacle, from start to finish, was nine months. What else of major significance typically takes about nine months?

If you were thinking of academic semesters, or school years, that would be true, but that's not a natural thing, but rather something constructed by human beings. But there's something in nature, at the essence of human life, that last nine months.

That's the gestation period for a baby. It typically takes nine months for a baby to be born after conception. So, if YAHUAH married the children of Israel in the wilderness and took the nation as His bride, that means that the product of their union, delivered nine months later, was the Tabernacle.

The Tabernacle of YAHUAH, where the Most High YAH would meet with the children of Israel for guidance, comfort, protection, and direction, was the baby of the union of YAH and His people. When YAHUAH married Israel, Israel as the bride conceived and delivered the tent of meeting, the Tabernacle. That meeting place reflected YAHUAH's glory in Heaven.

A cloud rested on the Tabernacle when they were to tarry at a certain place in their journeys. When YAHUAH decided the children of Israel could depart from a place, He lifted up the cloud. At night, a pillar of fire rested on the Tabernacle. The whole camp of Israel could see the cloud by day, or the fire by night.

The Tabernacle reflected the perfect worship of YAHUAH. The Father prescribed every detail. He had shown the original to Moses during their meeting of forty days and forty nights on Mount Sinai.

We will return to the details of the Tabernacle as we close out our meditations. But for now, it's important to recall that Moses was not the only prophet to see a vision of Heaven. Isaiah wrote about being ushered into Heaven in Isaiah 6. The Book of Ezekiel describes that prophet's vision of Heaven. And in 1 Kings 22, Micaiah also saw the court of Heaven.

David's Vision of the Temple

Most crucially, King David saw a vision of Heaven that transformed his whole life. I write about that in my second book, *Five Smooth Stones: David, The Man After YAH's Own Heart.* In that book, I discussed the subject as follows:

> The Most High appeared to David by the Holy Spirit in a way similar to how He appeared to Moses. 1 Chronicles 28 presents a small but dazzling nugget:
>
>> 11 Then David gave to Solomon his son the pattern of the porch, and of the houses thereof, and of the treasuries thereof, and of the upper chambers thereof, and of the inner parlours thereof, and of the place of the mercy seat,

> 12 And the pattern of all that he had ***by the spirit***, of the courts of the house of YAHUAH, and of all the chambers round about, of the treasuries of the house of ELOHIYM, and of the treasuries of the dedicated things:
>
> 13 Also for the courses of the priests and the Levites, and for all the work of the service of the house of YAHUAH, and for all the vessels of service in the house of YAHUAH (emphasis added).

David had a vision "***by the Spirit***." The Ruach ha Qodesh took the king to heaven and showed him His heavenly court, just as Moses ascended to heaven from Mount Sinai. Isaiah, in the sixth chapter of his book, also went to heaven. Similarly, YAHUAH showed heaven to Ezekiel. YAH also brought John to heaven to see His blazing throne room, as the Book of Revelation describes.[3]

At the end of his life, in 1 Chronicles 22:7, David recalled his fiery passion to build the temple: "***And David said to Solomon, My son, as for me, it was in my mind to build an house unto the name of YAHUAH my ELOHIYM.***"

The vision David received consumed his life. The Most High prevented the king from building the temple because he had killed so many people to conquer Israel's enemies. But while the Father refused to allow David to build the temple with his own hands, the son of Jesse received the vision, prepared the Temple's blueprints, and started getting things ready for the Temple's construction.

To prepare for the building process, David amassed what was likely the greatest fortune the world had ever seen. It consisted of one hundred thousand talents of gold, a million talents of silver, and untold millions of talents of bronze, brass, and other metals. The modern value of just the gold alone would have exceeded two hundred and four billion dollars in today's money. The silver would have been worth approximately $24 billion. All told, David likely amassed more than a quarter trillion dollars in today's money.

By comparison, the value of the gold held at Fort Knox as of 2018 came to just a little over $6 billion. From a per capita perspective, given Israel's size, the nation might have been the wealthiest nation in world history.

Finally, David commissioned his son Solomon as follows:

> Now set your heart and your soul to seek YAHUAH your ELOHIYM; arise therefore, and build ye the sanctuary of YAHUAH ELOHIYM, to bring the ark of the covenant of YAHUAH, and the holy vessels of ELOHIYM, into the house that is to be built to the name of YAHUAH.[4]

So why was the business of the Tabernacle and the Temple so important? Because YAHUAH's greatest priority is to manifest His glory. David explains briefly in Psalm 29: "***Give unto YAHUAH, O ye mighty, give unto YAHUAH glory and strength.***"[5] Psalm 29:9 continues, "***...and in his temple doth every one speak of his glory.***"

All who are possessed by the Most High's presence become preoccupied by His glory. All the holy angels, filled with His Ruach ha Qodesh, speak of YAH's glory. They don't speak of their own accomplishments. They don't talk about how great they are, or their fame, vacations, net worth, or possessions. Instead, the glory of YAHUAH utterly consumes them.

The Most High chose the children of Israel specifically to create a Tabernacle for Himself. This demand included the requirement for the people to order their lives with the perfect wisdom reflected in His laws, statutes and commandments. But YAHUAH did not merely seek an outward show of piety. Instead, He wanted the people to internalize His laws and obey His voice. In so doing, they would themselves be transformed into living tabernacles in which YAH could dwell.

We see this brought out in Revelation 21. There, we read these extraordinary words:

> And I heard a great voice out of heaven saying, Behold, the tabernacle of YAHUAH is with men, and he will dwell with them, and they shall be his people, and YAHUAH himself shall be with them, and be their ELOHIYM.[6]

The Father's great goal in creation is to turn Earth into His new home, just as Heaven has been. But it gets even deeper! YAH doesn't aim to live just on earth, but to live on earth INSIDE His people! Instead of being set apart from humanity, YAHUAH desires to dwell directly with and **IN** His chosen!

This critical insight, understood by the prophets such as Moses, David, and Isaiah, explains why YAHUSHA told His disciples, "***Neither shall they say, Lo here! or, lo there! for, behold, the kingdom of YAHUAH is within you.***"[7]

YAHUAH wanted a sacred people who, in community, would become His dwelling place. Even more fundamentally, ELOHIYM wanted each individual person to become His earthly house, or Tabernacle.

But how do we, as individuals, become tabernacles for the Most High? It all boils down to a single question, one that our Master YAHUSHA posed to Peter at the end of John's gospel. It is the same question that YAHUAH puts to all His servants throughout history. This book will show how some of YAH's chosen vessels came to terms with this most fundamental of questions.

Prayer for the Tabernacle

Heavenly Father, thank You for all Your goodness toward Your inheritance. Please show us Your glory! Make Your people, and make ME, Your tabernacle. Fill me with Your Spirit and Your presence. Live in me for Your praise. In YAHUSHA's holy name, so be it. Thank You, Father! HalleluYAH!

Chapter 2, "Lovest Thou Me?"

One question defines all the stories, parables, and people of the Bible. Everything organizes itself around this question. The Father poses it to everyone. And in turn, His Son, YAHUSHA HA MASHIACH, posed the question to Peter in John 21:15: "***Lovest thou me more than these?***"[8]

This question is two thousand years old. But it's also brand new, because it is being posed to everyone who desires to be saved, to enter into covenant with the Father through His Son.

In sum, YAHUSHA asked Peter if His disciple loved the Master more than the things of this world. To highlight its importance, the Messiah posed it to Peter three times. Three is the number of completeness and harmony in Scripture.

The Son of David asked Peter whether the disciple loved Messiah more than Peter's occupation as a fisherman, his earthly wealth, or his family and friends. ***Peter, YAHUSHA asked, do you love Me more than anything in the world?***

Or maybe we can frame it in a slightly different way: Is there anything that you love MORE than YAHUSHA? Do you love your bank account, house, car, spouse, or children more than the King of Glory? Are you willing to give up everything to follow the Master wherever He goes? Will you do whatever He calls you to do?

Losing Your Life

Every disciple must answer this question for herself or himself. YAHUSHA repeats this theme throughout the gospels. For instance, in Luke 9:24, Messiah warns His disciples, "***For whosoever will save his life shall lose it: but whosoever will lose his life for my sake, the same shall save it.***"

In this passage, He plainly states that you have to be willing to give up everything for YAHUSHA in order to save your soul. If there's anything more important to you than the Son of David, you will lose your soul.

Here's the odd thing: you think that you're saving your soul by making the Messiah second place to whatever you feel is more important than Him. However, you're only cementing your doom and proving your unworthiness for eternal life in the Son.

Losing Your Life: the Covid-19 Vaccine

The most obvious modern day example of YAHUSHA's principle in Luke 9:24 is the Covid-19 vaccine. Billions of people thought they were saving their lives by following the so-called science. They didn't have the spiritual insight to see that the vaccine was a product from hell. They were not curious enough to study and research it.

Had they researched the vaccine with as much energy as they research their dinner plans, or which cable plan they will procure, or into what school they will enroll their children, they might have discovered that the vaccine was created with fallen angel technology. A little Internet research might have helped them see that the vaccine was created to alter the recipients' DNA, and change them from human beings to entities marked forever to the Beast who gave it.

In other words, those who voluntarily took the vaccine, whether out of fear of losing their lives from Covid, or fear of losing their jobs, voluntarily took the mark of the Beast. They must now confront everything that Revelation 13 and 14 say about the mark.

These people have agreed with Satan, and his satanic life and energy course through their bodies. That is why so many millions of people have already died or been permanently disabled by the so-called medication. Instead of helping people, it's killing people. But again, that's what the father of lies does: he kills, steals, and destroys. Why would the Covid vaccine be any different?

Those who took the Covid vaccine, and all similar technologies, like the new mRNA cancer vaccines that are currently being released, have taken the mark of the Beast. They feared for their lives, but that is exactly what they have thrown away.

Loving Father or Mother More

YAHUSHA offers many other teachings to explain that we must love Him more than anything else in this world. One such teaching is found in Matthew 10:37-39:

> 37 He that loveth father or mother more than me is not worthy of me: and he that loveth son or daughter more than me is not worthy of me.
>
> 38 And he that taketh not his cross, and followeth after me, is not worthy of me.
>
> 39 He that findeth his life shall lose it: and he that loseth his life for my sake shall find it.[9]

What YAHUSHA teaches here could not be clearer: if you love anyone more than you love Him, then you are not worthy of Him. If you refuse to follow the hard, lonely, and narrow road of life in the Messiah, then you are not worthy of Him.

All who try to "find" their lives will lose them. What does that mean? It means that anyone whose foremost concern is trying to do a good job for the sake of earthly success will lose their souls. They don't have to hate people outwardly, or be axe murderers, serial killers, or deeply immoral people.

It's actually much more insidious: all they have to do is not think about what the God Who created them requires of them. Instead, they focus their whole attention on what it takes to be a good employee, or a good wife, or a good husband, or a good parent, without devoting much thought to what YAHUAH wants from them, or why He created them in the first place.

The One Who created everything is posing a very specific, very clear question to each and every one us: Are you loving YAHUAH more than anything else in your life? Is there anything you love MORE than the Most High?

What are some of these things you might love more than YAHUAH? Here are a few:

- A good job
- A large net worth
- A nice house
- A beautiful wife, or handsome husband
- Your children
- Prestige in your social clubs, like fraternities or sororities
- Your expensive car
- Your parents, or other family members
- Your free time and leisure
- Your respect in the eyes of your community

If you would sacrifice your devotion to YAHUAH for any of these things, then you do not love YAHUAH "***more than these***." That choice, whether you make it intentionally or unintentionally, has eternal consequences.

This is a tricky subject. On the surface, it is praiseworthy to love and respect one's parents and family members. The fourth commandment is a warning to honor your father and mother. And we need to do all we can to love and honor them. But our devotion to our parents needs to ALWAYS take second place to our devotion to YAHUAH.

In Luke 14:26, Messiah put it this way:

> If any man come to me, and hate not his father, and mother, and wife, and children, and brethren, and sisters, yea, and his own life also, he cannot be my disciple.

The love that we have for YAHUSHA has to be so deep and intense that our love for our parents or family members almost seems like hatred by comparison. The Son of David did not urge us to hate our family members to sow needless division. Instead, He is saying that we should be able to sacrifice absolutely everything and everyone for His sake.

If our parents have rejected the Most High, even after prayers, warnings and pleadings, then we have no business violating ABBA's instructions to us concerning how we deal with them. We have to follow our Heavenly Father, even if it means turning away from those with whom we grew up.

Wide Way Versus Strait Gate

In Matthew 7:13-14, the Messiah gives another teaching on how we should love Him more than the things of the world:

> 13 Enter ye in at the strait gate: for wide is the gate, and broad is the way, that leadeth to destruction, and many there be which go in thereat:

> 14 Because strait is the gate, and narrow is the way, which leadeth unto life, and few there be that find it.[10]

YAHUSHA urges His followers to enter into the kingdom through the "strait," or the narrow gate, instead of through the broad and wide way. What does this mean?

To walk the wide or broad way means that a person lives his or life without much focus on the Father and His will. You may spend a little time thinking about the Bible, or YAHUSHA. But you're equally occupied with things of the world. This broad road does not have to be filled with evil things. It just means that you are not focused on Messiah and His will for your life if it inconveniences you in any way.

We see illustrations of this when we look at people who attend church and profess a faith in Messiah but who still engage in worldly things. People follow the broad road when they are more passionate about sports, or other entertainments, than they are about the Messiah. These people are not moved to read the Bible for themselves even for five minutes. But they have no problem watching a three hour ball game. In fact, they can spend the entire weekend watching sports, one game after the next, but never have time to read the Bible or pray to YAHUAH.

Another way to walk the broad road is to fill your mind with making money, instead of serving the Father. YAHUSHA condemned this also in Matthew 6:24:

> No man can serve two masters: for either he will hate the one, and love the other; or else he will hold to the one, and despise the other. Ye cannot serve YAHUAH and mammon.

The "***strait gate***" is that path of life that makes everything take second place to serving the Father. For those entering YAHUAH's kingdom through the strait gate, they are willing to give up anything if it keeps them from doing what YAHUSHA demands. For these people, nothing is more important to them than serving YAHUAH, exactly as YAHUAH demands.

Entering the narrow way may make one look silly to those who don't follow it. In fact, people might not like you EVEN when you don't say a word. How do they know that you're following the narrow way? Because they can spiritually SEE it on you. They KNOW that you have devoted yourself to YAHUSHA. They KNOW that you belong to the Father. You look different to them. It's as if there is a light in you and on you, just as there was a light on Moses' face after He visited with YAHUAH on Mount Sinai.

Being in the presence of YAHUAH makes you hunger to be in His presence even more. Spending time with Him transforms you, and puts a spiritual light on you that people in the world can see even when you cannot.

When you follow the narrow way, you won't be able to do everything that your family members and friends do. You may not be able to go to the holiday party or to the family cookout, because you don't want to be defiled by the music, the food, the jokes, the atmosphere of the wicked. It may lead to loneliness. YAHUSHA's friendship and presence, however, are sweeter and more valuable than the friendship of people who hate YAHUAH. Ultimately, they hate you, too.

How do you know they hate both the Most High and you? Because the Master told us, in John 15:20: "***Remember the word that I said unto you, The servant is not greater than his lord. If they have persecuted me, they will also persecute you.***"

In dealing with the loneliness of the narrow road, it helps to remind ourselves who it is from whom we are walking away. These are wicked people, even if they call themselves our mother or father, or brother or sister, or so-called friends or co-workers.

Even before you reject them, they have already rejected not only you, but also your Father in Heaven. YAHUSHA Himself taught how to think about flesh-and-blood family:

> 48 But he answered and said unto him that told him, Who is my mother? and who are my brethren?
>
> 49 And he stretched forth his hand toward his disciples, and said, Behold my mother and my brethren!
>
> 50 For whosoever shall do the will of my Father which is in heaven, the same is my brother, and sister, and mother.[11]

The Master expressly rejected His flesh and blood as His family. Instead, He said that those who "***shall do the will of my Father which is in heaven, the same is my brother, and sister, and mother.***" True family follows and obeys YAHUAH, whether or not they are flesh and blood.

One of the greatest struggles in following YAHUSHA is the realization that the overwhelming number of people we know in life do NOT follow YAHUSHA. They may go to church every time the church doors open, but they likely hate YAHUAH. Most people hate YAHUAH.

It's not our job to do anything but obey the Master's voice and do His will in our lives. We must love Him more than we love the people and things around us. It won't make us popular. We will have a lonely journey. Most won't make it, even most of our family and friends. But following the narrow way will lead to eternal life.

Almost There: The Rich Ruler

During His ministry, YAHUSHA met a man who seemed intensely interested in the narrow way. He said all the right stuff to make it seem like he loved the Father "***more than these.***"

> 17 And when he was gone forth into the way, there came one running, and kneeled to him, and asked him, Good Master, what shall I do that I may inherit eternal life?
>
> 18 And YAHUSHA said unto him, Why callest thou me good? there is none good but one, that is, ELOHIYM.
>
> 19 Thou knowest the commandments, Do not commit adultery, Do not kill, Do not steal, Do not

> bear false witness, Defraud not, Honour thy father and mother.
>
> 20 And he answered and said unto him, Master, all these have I observed from my youth.
>
> 21 Then YAHUSHA beholding him loved him, and said unto him, One thing thou lackest: go thy way, sell whatsoever thou hast, and give to the poor, and thou shalt have treasure in heaven: and come, take up the cross, and follow me.
>
> 22 And he was sad at that saying, and went away grieved: for he had great possessions.[12]

This rich ruler approached YAHUSHA, which is a great start. He acknowledged to the Master His holiness, that He was good, and earnestly inquired about how to obtain eternal life. He listened carefully to His teachings, and had apparently been following YAHUSHA fairly closely, even if from a distance.

But the Messiah knows all men's hearts. He knew what the ruler loved more than anything: his wealth. So YAHUSHA commanded the man to sell his possessions, give the proceeds to the poor, and follow Him.

The man turned away and departed from the Messiah, filled with grief. Under no circumstances, the ruler thought to himself, would he EVER give up his wealth. Instead, he wanted an easy salvation, a salvation as a side to the main entrée of a great life with lots of money. He viewed his money as more important than his soul.

How many people think that one's relationship with the Father is a "***nice-to-have***," but money, relationships, entertainments, or prestige are "***must-haves***?" All too many adopt this view. This wealthy man showed the classic case of the "It don't take all that" religion that fills most homes and churches today.

The rich man thought he could have YAHUSHA PLUS. Plus what? Plus **anything**! YAHUSHA plus social prominence. Or YAHUSHA plus great degrees, great neighborhoods, great fame. In this case, it was YAHUSHA plus lots of money.

But we are called to a narrow road. We can't have YAHUSHA plus ANYTHING! Yes, the Father might be pleased, as we will see with Abraham, to give us back what we offer to Him. But we have to offer it to Him first. A small number of believers can follow YAHUSHA and have great wealth. But most of us won't. Most of us must give up our pretensions to the great things in life in order to follow our Heavenly Father.

The rich man departed from Messiah, and followed the broad road. He didn't even know he was on the broad road, but that's exactly where he ended up.

The scary thing about the broad road is that you don't have to intend to follow it: you just have to hold onto something, anything, just a little harder than you hold onto YAHUAH. The rich ruler may not even have been aware that he had abandoned YAHUSHA. Maybe he just imagined that he would have more time. Maybe he thought he would come back to Messiah a little later.

Whether he knew it or not, he followed the broad road. He did not love YAHUSHA "***more than these.***"

The Master knew that the man rejected the narrow road because he lacked two things from a spiritual perspective: focus and toughness.

Spiritual Violence

YAHUSHA knew that the only way someone can be focused on Him, and willing to lose his or life for Messiah's sake, was if they developed a mental focus and toughness. They had to start talking to themselves about what YAHUAH demanded.

The Son of David explained this in Matthew 11:12, saying, "***And from the days of John the Baptist until now the kingdom of heaven suffereth violence, and the violent take it by force.***"

YAHUSHA uses very precise imagery here. The phrase translated "***suffereth violence***" carries the thought of catching up and carrying something away with force. To put this another way, to inherit the kingdom, you have to be like an eagle looking for prey.

One who wants to win the kingdom has to be focused like a laser on that prey. He or she has to swoop in and snatch that prey off the ground. The little rabbit or dog shouldn't stand a chance against the eagle, because the eagle watched the prey from a distance, and developed a strategy to carry it away for dinner. When eagles or hawks capture their victims, they leave nothing to chance, and they watch the prey for long periods of time. They think about the prey, and they apply all of their powers to getting it. They think about and strategize how to deploy the optimal combination of force, wind sailing, physics, and victim emotion to win that battle.

We must be like the eagle in order to enter the kingdom. The saints must be violent about pursuing YAHUAH and His Son. We have to not care whether people call us crazy, or question our choices, as long as those choices are driven by the Word of YAHUAH and His commandments.

True saints will develop a mental toughness. They'll mourn the loneliness, and then they'll fight it. Those who follow YAHUAH remind themselves constantly that they have to fight through the loneliness to win YAHUSHA and everlasting life. They remind themselves, every day if needed, that it will all be worth it in the end. And they carefully consider the future fate of those who don't take these steps to put on their spiritual armor and fight.

The Messiah put this a different way in John 4:34, where He told His disciples, "***My meat is to do the will of him that sent me, and to finish his work.***" YAHUSHA was teaching His disciples that doing the commandments of His Father YAHUAH was even more important than eating and nourishing His body. He focused on obeying His Heavenly Father more than anything else.

The 144,000: Following the Lamb

To love YAHUSHA "***more than these***" means at least one other thing: it means that you will follow the Lamb wherever He goes. Revelation 14 describes the special remnant who follow YAHUSHA.

> 1 And I looked, and, lo, a Lamb stood on the mount Sion, and with him an hundred forty and four thousand, having his Father's name written in their foreheads.
>
> 2 And I heard a voice from heaven, as the voice of many waters, and as the voice of a great thunder: and I heard the voice of harpers harping with their harps:
>
> 3 And they sung as it were a new song before the throne, and before the four beasts, and the elders: and no man could learn that song but the hundred and forty and four thousand, which were redeemed from the earth.
>
> 4 These are they which were not defiled with women; for they are virgins. These are they which follow the Lamb whithersoever he goeth. These were redeemed from among men, being the firstfruits unto YAHUAH and to the Lamb.[13]

This special remnant is characterized by four traits. First, the remnant has the "***Father's name written in their foreheads.***" Ezekiel 9:4 gives the precept upon which Revelation 14:1 is based:

> And YAHUAH said unto him, Go through the midst of the city, through the midst of Jerusalem, and set a mark upon the foreheads of the men that

> sigh and that cry for all the abominations that be done in the midst thereof.[14]

To have the Father's name written upon one's forehead means that ABBA's laws, statutes and commandments are engraved in a person's thinking. David says the same thing in Psalm 1:2, when he describes the "blessed man" in this way: "***But his delight is in the law of YAHUAH, and in his law doth he meditate day and night.***" No matter the trial or circumstance, a true saint will be digesting Torah, meditating on Scripture, applying the Bible's life principles to his or her own life.

Those who follow the Lamb are obsessed with the Most High. People may scorn them by saying, "It doesn't take all that." But the followers of the Lamb will always disagree. They are radical, and maniacally focused on their Father's will. They are determined to let Him live in them through His Set Apart Spirit. They want to carry and dwell in His presence at all times.

This hunger for YAH's presence is the reason why Moses told the Most High, "***If thy presence go not with me, carry us not up hence.***"[15] True followers of YAHUAH talk frequently with Him, and can't bear to face any situation without His presence with them.

Second, they sing "***a new song.***" This means that they go through excruciatingly painful experiences. Those who lead light and easy lives often have little need to sing, because they haven't faced trials that bring joy at the end. We sing new songs when we go through tough experiences, and YAHUAH's Ruach fills and guides us in singing our song of triumphing over adversity.

Third, the followers of the Lamb are not defiled with "woman," or the state of woman. This is not speaking primarily of sexual abstinence, although that might be a part of the text's meaning. More specifically, the devoted followers of the Lamb are those who are not defiled by "***the woman***," meaning, the "***whore of Babylon***," the spirit of Satan which moves everyone who has not devoted herself or himself to the Father.

Since Messiah rose from the dead, the woman has presented herself as the Gentile church, because the churches counterfeit the ways and teachings of YAH in Scripture. Revelation 17:3 further describes the woman as "***sit[ting] upon a scarlet coloured beast, full of names of blasphemy, having seven heads and ten horns.***"

The woman is not just the church, but also the world. She is the flesh operating under the power and force of the Beast, opposing YAHUAH and His purposes. Every single person who is not filled with YAHUAH's Ruach fights against Him, even if they don't know or believe it.

The people in the one hundred and forty-four thousand are those who are pure from the stain of the world. John urges this group in 1 John 5:21: "***Little children, keep yourselves from idols.***" James also comments, "***Pure religion and undefiled before ELOHIYM and the Father is this, To visit the fatherless and widows in their affliction, and to keep himself unspotted from the world.***"[16]

Those who are virgins, in this sense, are those who are not spotted or defiled by the world. Because they are pure of the world's hold, they are free to "***follow the Lamb whithersoever he goeth.***"[17]

In other words, the chosen of the Father follow the Lamb wherever He goes. They are the people who love YAHUSHA "***more than these.***" They are relentless, focused, and narrow. They let nothing and no one in their lives keep them from following YAHUAH and His Son YAHUSHA.

Now that we have looked briefly at what it means to love the Most High YAH "***more than these,***" let's see how this plays out in the lives of a few heroes of the faith. We start with Abraham, the friend of YAH.

Chapter 3, Abraham

"And Abraham stretched forth his hand, and took the knife to slay his son."
-Genesis 22:10

He must have smiled as he watched his dictator-king, his adopted son, enslave one people after the next. Nimrod had halted the steady population migration that the Most High had commanded Noah and his sons. So soon after the Flood, when people still feared to follow the fallen angels, the son of Cush gleefully pushed witchcraft, divination, and enchantments. Nimrod sprinkled these spiritual toxins over the land like glitter, and reimposed the worship of the old gods.

No one, Satan thought to himself, would be able to walk untainted through Nimrod's empire that crawled over the planet like a creeping cancer. No one would survive under Hillel's sun, or breathe his air, without prostrating themselves to his servants Inanna, Ningal, Enki, and the myriad other angels ravenously collecting worship from the hapless people under Nimrod's rule.

We can only imagine how stunned Satan stood as he watched his once-faithful Inanna worshiper, Abram, respond to this chilling speech from the Most High El:

> 1 Now YAHUAH had said unto Abram, Get thee
> out of thy country, and from thy kindred, and from
> thy father's house, unto a land that I will shew thee:

> 2 And I will make of thee a great nation, and I will bless thee, and make thy name great; and thou shalt be a blessing:
>
> 3 And I will bless them that bless thee, and curse him that curseth thee: and in thee shall all families of the earth be blessed.[18]

The words chilled Satan's heart. The Most High El had told Abram to leave almost everyone and everything he knew. This included his beloved Inanna and all the gods. The property and wealth, prestige and prominence. The blood sacrifices. But even more disheartening to the devil was Abram's ungrateful, horrible reply. The son of Terah, one of the first citizens of Ur of the Chaldees, had the gall to believe YAHUAH! In Genesis 12:4, we read Abram's response:

> 4 So Abram departed, as YAHUAH had spoken unto him; and Lot went with him: and Abram was seventy and five years old when he departed out of Haran.[19]

Satan had gambled that Abram's idolatry would disqualify the man from service. But Hillel could not have been more wrong. YAHUAH is able to turn the greatest idolaters, and the most defiled sinners, into His most devoted servants.

Departing from Ur, Loving Him More

Obeying the Most High's voice, Abram packed his things, gathered his wife Sarai and his nephew Lot, and left all the glories of his possessions, position, and prestige in Ur of the Chaldees. Abram had been as firmly entrenched in all the ways of Babylon as his fellow

Chaldeans. However, when he heard YAHUAH's call, he responded.

That single act of obedience changed history forever.

Oh, let's not get it twisted, Abram was not perfect. He brought Lot with him, in direct contradiction to the Most High's command to "***Get thee . . . from thy kindred.***" Abram had compassion on his nephew after the boy's father had died. He stubbornly maintained his commitment to watch over Lot.

This would one day prove a costly mistake for Abram. Sometimes, our faithfulness to our earthly family, or to fallen codes of conduct rather than Torah, can cause us to be unfaithful to the Father's commands.

But YAHUAH overcame even that sin, and blessed Abram's obedience and willing spirit. This act of leaving all that he knew and loved was Abram's answer to the Most High's implied question, "***Lovest thou Me more than these?***"

Interceding for Lot, Loving Him More

Abraham obeyed the Heavenly Father's call in many ways. For instance, Abraham's great love for Lot extended to the man even after the latter chose to move to Sodom, a city of great evil. The Father described the city like this: "***But the men of Sodom were wicked and sinners before YAHUAH exceedingly.***"[20] Lot "***pitched his tent toward Sodom,***" because the plain of Jordan was well-watered everywhere, a place where enterprising farmers could make a killing with vibrant crops.[21]

Lot knew the people of Sodom were evil. He knew who these people were when he first went. But he didn't care, because he wanted that money. As the young people might say, Lot wanted that bag, and wanted to make that paper.

Lot went into an evil place, and found himself accommodating evil. As Lot grew his family, he selected an unbeliever as a wife, and despite his own faith in YAHUAH, he failed to pass it down to his wife or to any of his children.

Judgment drew near to Sodom and Gomorrah, but Lot couldn't see it because of his greed. Abraham, who followed the Most High far more closely than his nephew, heard directly from YAHUAH about the coming judgment.

> 20 And YAHUAH said, Because the cry of Sodom and Gomorrah is great, and because their sin is very grievous;
>
> 21 I will go down now, and see whether they have done altogether according to the cry of it, which is come unto me; and if not, I will know.[22]

YAHUAH told Abraham He was preparing to judge Sodom and Gomorrah. In response, Lot's uncle immediately prayed and interceded for the cities. Why did he do this? Because he knew that his nephew lived there, and he wanted to protect him.

But even the way that Abraham pled with the Father showed something very powerful. As he began his prayer, Abraham asked for the entire city to be spared from destruction if fifty righteous people were found there. The Most High agreed to this petition.

From there, Abraham kept going down until he reached ten righteous people. He prayed that YAHUAH would spare the city if ten righteous were to be found, a request to which the Most High agreed.

At that point, YAHUAH departed from Abraham. But why did the prophet stop at ten righteous, as opposed to running all the way down to a single righteous person? Because Abraham imagined that Lot was more righteous than he was. Despite knowing Lot's greed, the older man expected that Lot would have at least, like himself, converted his own family.

Lot had a wife, so there were two people right there. He had four adult daughters, two of which were married, bringing the total to eight. Each of the adult daughters likely had at least one child. That comes to ten. Abraham expected that, with those ten people, there would be the minimum number of righteous people who could permit the city to be spared. He thought this because he imagined that Lot had raised his family in the same way that Abraham had raised his family: in belief and trust of YAHUAH ELOHIYM.

But Abraham was wrong. From all of the available evidence, NONE of the family in Lot's sphere of influence followed the Most High. When the angels came to rescue Lot because of Abraham's prayers, his two sons-in-law laughed at Lot's testimony, and perished in Sodom's destruction. Disobeying YAH's command, Lot's wife turned back to see the judgment and was turned into a pillar of stone. But that cascade of losses did not end there for Lot.

His two single daughters each date-raped their father to continue the line, creating two of the most evil lineages to ever plague the earth, the Ammonites and the Moabites. Both of them have persecuted the chosen people for centuries, right up to today.

The only one to make it out alive, whose faith was intact, was Lot himself. But he had no testimony, or anything good and tangible to show for himself.

In Abraham's intercession and love for his family, he stopped at ten righteous. He did not fight or argue with the Most High. The next morning, he looked out to the horizon and watched the plumes of smoke ascend from Sodom, Gomorrah, and the other cities of the plain. Even in seeing this, he did not argue with YAH. Abraham calmly accepted the Father's verdict.

In humbly submitting to YAHUAH's judgment, Abraham loved YAHUAH more than he loved even his own family.

Separation From the World Brings Blessing

One more quick item here demands attention. As we read earlier, in Genesis 12, the Most High had commanded Abraham to depart not only from Ur, but also from Lot and his other family members. Abraham did not obey this last command because of his devotion to Lot.

However, because of the great wealth each amassed in their journeys, Abraham and Lot had to separate. When Lot finally moved to Sodom, something very special happened. The Scriptures tell us,

> 14 And YAHUAH said unto Abram, after that Lot was separated from him, Lift up now thine eyes, and look from the place where thou art northward, and southward, and eastward, and westward.[23]

When you read between the lines in this verse, you see something very intriguing: the Most High had stopped speaking to Abraham. It was only when Lot separated from Abraham that YAHUAH began to speak again. He reaffirmed His promise to the son of Terah, commanding him to lift up his eyes, and promising possession of all that he surveyed. In response, Abram built an altar and worshipped YAHUAH.

When we disobey the Father, no matter the reason, He may stop speaking to us until we fully comply with His last command. Have you reached a barren point in your life? Look back over what the Most High has told you to do. Have you obeyed everything? If not, return to that point of disobedience, and obey Him. Obedience always unleashes blessings. It did for Abraham, and it does the same for us, Abraham's children.

Isaac the Promised Child, Loving Him More

In one final, awe-inspiring way, Abraham demonstrated a fierce devotion to the Father that transcended all his earthly passions and loves. As he journeyed, Abraham continued to win wealth and respect in the lands of Canaan, Egypt, and the Philistines. But he had no heir to whom to bequeath his fortune, and to see the fulfilment of YAHUAH's promises to Him.

Despite his fortune, his heart longed for the promised son and heir. Abraham had successfully led his entire household in love and devotion to YAHUAH, but remained childless.

Despite having witnessed to kings, including Pharaoh in Egypt, testifying about YAHUAH, Abraham remained without a son and heir.

While Abraham and Sarah went through many trials, and some sinful failures, they finally rejoiced to see the promised child, Isaac. Sarah was ninety, well past child-bearing age, and Abraham was one hundred years old.

This was the child they had waited for their entire lives. For twenty-five years, ABBA YAHUAH had promised an heir, and now he had finally arrived. The household rejoiced for the miraculous birth of Isaac.

The child grew up to be strong and wise like his father. But then, ABBA did the unthinkable: He commanded Abraham to sacrifice the child of promise:

> 1 And it came to pass after these things, that ELOHIYM did tempt Abraham, and said unto him, Abraham: and he said, Behold, here I am.
>
> 2 And he said, Take now thy son, thine only son Isaac, whom thou lovest, and get thee into the land of Moriah; and offer him there for a burnt offering upon one of the mountains which I will tell thee of.[24]

The Most High commanded Abraham to take the child of promise and sacrifice him back to YAHUAH. The couple had waited a quarter century, and only received Isaac through prayer and supernatural intervention. Now, the Father wanted him to give up the very promise for which they had waited so long?

Yes, that was **exactly** what YAHUAH demanded. And that is exactly what Abraham did.

We read nothing of Abraham weeping and wailing, protesting, arguing, or fussing with the Most High. In the next verse, Scripture tells us,

> 3 And Abraham rose up early in the morning, and saddled his ass, and took two of his young men with him, and Isaac his son, and clave the wood for the burnt offering, and rose up, and went unto the place of which ELOHIYM had told him.[25]

Abraham simply obeyed. He not only obeyed, but he did so IMMEDIATELY. He rose up the very next morning, and early in the morning at that. Abraham, Isaac and two of his servants journeyed together to Mount Moriah to make the offering. They brought no animal offering with them except for Isaac.

When Isaac asked where the offering was, Abraham replied with unshakeable faith, "***My son, ELOHIYM will provide himself a lamb for a burnt offering: so they went both of them together.***"[26] Abraham knew, deep down in his bones, that the Father would provide the offering, whether it was Isaac himself or a lamb.

When they arrived at the place the Father directed, Abraham built an altar, and then bound his son Isaac, the way he had bound lambs for offerings. Parenthetically, Isaac was not a little child at this point: he was at least a teenager, and possibly a young man in his late teens or early twenties. Having grown up with his father's strong faith in YAHUAH, Isaac willingly submitted himself to be offered up to the Father.

Finally, Abraham "***stretched forth his hand, and took the knife to slay his son.***"[27] Abraham did not deny the Father what He asked for: he prepared to kill his son as an offering to his Heavenly Father, because that is what YAHUAH asked for of him.

Abraham exhibited perfect faith. He believed, even if he had to actually go through with it and kill Isaac, that the Most High would raise his son from the dead.

This was the patriarch's final great test. YAHUAH sent His angel to stop him from bringing down his knife into his son's chest:

> 12 And he said, Lay not thine hand upon the lad, neither do thou any thing unto him: for now I know

> that thou fearest ELOHIYM, seeing thou hast not withheld thy son, thine only son from me.[28]

Why did the Most High commend Abraham in this story? What was the exercise all about? YAHUAH called the man to kill his son to show Him, and the whole world, that Abraham feared YAH. The son of Terah feared YAHUAH with such fierce devotion that he would not withhold even the child of promise, whom Abraham loved more than life itself. In other words, by this act of devotion, Abraham proved, once and for all, that he loved YAHUAH "***more than these.***" Abraham held absolutely nothing back from YAH.

Because Abraham gave Isaac back to YAHUAH, the Most High in turn gave the child back to Abraham. The Heavenly Father even gave a ram in the thicket as an offering.

Abraham demonstrated perfect devotion, and became the father of many nations, and the father of the faith in YAHUAH. All who trusted in the Most High after Abraham would come under Abraham's spiritual bloodline.

This is why Genesis 15:6 tells us that Abraham "***believed in YAHUAH; and he counted it to him for righteousness.***" In Romans 4:16, Paul calls Abraham "***the father of us all,***" because Abraham believed YAHUAH, becoming the template and pattern for all who believe.

Do you believe in YAHUAH and His Son as Abraham did? Would you have offered up your child, whatever that child is, if He asked for it? Or would you have kept it back?

That child might not be a physical child at all: it might be your job, your marriage, your family members, or your friends. Your sacrifice might be that country club membership or prestigious existence you've worked a lifetime to obtain. Or perhaps your Isaac is your net worth or assets, or your house or cars. Whatever it is that the Father asks you to surrender to Him, you should do it. And you should do it now, while there's still time.

Abraham became the father of all who believe in YAHUAH because he proved, beyond any doubt, that he loved YAHUAH "***more than these.***" He faced and passed the test.

His test wasn't without sacrifice. When Sarah died, in Genesis 23, she and Abraham were not living together. He lived in Beersheba, and she lived in Kiriath-Arba. They were about 30 miles apart, which would have been a couple days' journey from one another. Abraham's devotion to the Most High might have cost him his marriage. Whenever you follow Him, people will leave you, sometimes even people who like to think they also follow YAH.

May ABBA empower us to live like Abraham, and love YAHUAH more than these things of the world!

Chapter 4, Moses

Few people ever walked more closely with YAHUAH than Moses. In many ways, he was THE giant of human history. David rivaled him in his devotion to YAHUAH and achievements, but Moses was the great prophet after whom YAHUSHA HA MASHIACH would pattern Himself.

But Moses also paints a complex portrait. It's one much more contradictory than our simple children's Bible stories suggest.

Moses himself did not live to bring the children of Israel out of the wilderness and into the promised land of Canaan. Why was this? Moses didn't make it because he struck the rock instead of speaking to it, as Numbers 20:11 describes.

Speak to the Rock, Or Strike It?

Moses died over a paragraph and a stick. How did that happen?

After Moses led the children of Israel out of Egypt, he spent forty long years pastoring a nation at war with him. Despite all the miracles that the people witnessed and experienced through his hand, the people never wearied of murmuring and complaining.

They complained about the lack of food. They complained about the lack of water. They complained about not having enough seasonings to their liking. They complained about not having idols to worship as in Egypt. In short, they complained about everything.

And they wore Moses out. They wore out his LAST nerve.

In the final episode, recounted in Numbers 20, the people cried and whined about not having enough water. But the old prophet had been here before. The first time this happened, forty years earlier, ABBA had commanded Moses to strike the rock with his staff. When he did that, water gushed out from the rock supernaturally. It was enough water to quench the thirst of millions of people.

This time, however, ABBA gave Moses a new command: speak to the rock, rather than striking it. So what did Moses do? He struck the rock, twice for good measure, after calling the people a group of rebels.

Psalm 106 well summarizes the sordid episode:

> 32 They angered him also at the waters of strife, so that it went ill with Moses for their sakes:
>
> 33 Because they provoked his spirit, so that he spake unadvisedly with his lips.[29]

In Moses' anger, he spoke things he should not have spoken. He also disobeyed YAHUAH's direct command. But how did the great prophet get to the breaking point. Was it merely because of the disobedience of the people?

We can find the true root of Moses' problem long before this episode at the end of his life. We can turn all the way back to the beginning of their time in the wilderness, decades earlier.

Wilding Out In the Wilderness

Exodus 32 tells the tale. About four months after departing Egypt, Moses communed with YAHUAH in the mountaintop for forty day and forty nights. Having been gone for over a month, the chronically impatient and evil Israelites urged Aaron, Moses' brother, to make other gods for them to worship in Moses' absence. To oblige the people, Aaron fashioned a golden calf. This idol represented a violation of the very first commandments the Most High gave to the people.

As Moses worshipped YAHUAH, the people danced and participated in debauchery before the fallen angels that YAH had just vanquished. As Moses worshipped, the Most High took a hard right turn and stopped. He revealed to His prophet exactly what the people were doing. He described the idolatry, and even told Moses the very words that the people were saying to one another. These were all things that Moses could not possibly have known on his own. There were no cellphone cameras, Internet, or social media. It was just YAHUAH and Moses.

The Most High then gave a very specific command to His servant:

> 9 And YAHUAH said unto Moses, I have seen this people, and, behold, it is a stiffnecked people:
>
> 10 Now therefore let me alone, that my wrath may wax hot against them, and that I may consume them: and I will make of thee a great nation.[30]

After explaining His views of the people, YAHUAH then urged Moses to leave Him alone, or to stop interceding on the people's behalf. What was the Most High really telling Moses to do? He was asking the prophet to offer the people back to Moses, and to defer to the Holy One's judgment as to how to handle them. YAHUAH told Moses that it was His ***determination*** that the best way to handle the apostasy of the people was through their ***extermination***.

So, consider this scene again from a slightly different angle. ABBA had miraculously given the children of Israel to Moses as a gift. The son of Amram had longed for Israel's deliverance for more than four decades. He finally received it. And now, after all the pain and agony he endured in confronting Pharaoh, and even his own people, he was being told to offer the people back to YAH for Him to deal with them.

In other words, Moses was being ordered by the King of Glory to stop praying for a stiff-necked people. YAH wanted to consume the people and start over with Moses. Why him? Because Moses was a humble and righteous man, like Abraham before him.

Moses' Uncalled For Intercession

What did Moses think about YAHUAH's command? Let's look at the next verses to see.

> 11 And Moses besought YAHUAH his ELOHIYM, and said, YAHUAH, why doth thy wrath wax hot against thy people, which thou hast brought forth out of the land of Egypt with great power, and with a mighty hand?
>
> 12 Wherefore should the Egyptians speak, and say, For mischief did he bring them out, to slay them in the mountains, and to consume them from the face of the earth? Turn from thy fierce wrath, and repent of this evil against thy people.
>
> 13 Remember Abraham, Isaac, and Israel, thy servants, to whom thou swarest by thine own self, and saidst unto them, I will multiply your seed as the stars of heaven, and all this land that I have spoken of will I give unto your seed, and they shall inherit it for ever.[31]

Moses delivered a mix of replies. First, he immediately starts to intercede in prayer for the House of Israel. This is exactly the opposite of what YAHUAH had instructed Moses to do. The next question he asks is one that the Most High had already answered: namely, *Why is YAH mad with the people*? But YAHUAH had already told His prophet why He was mad: the nation was stiff-necked, unbelieving, and idolatrous. They immediately broke YAH's covenant. In response, the Most High wanted to wipe them out in order to start over with Moses.

Moses next does something positive: he recites back to the Father His mighty acts in delivering Israel.

The prophet approaches the Most High with the respect of someone who recognizes YAHUAH's greatness and glory. The former shepherd wrongfully tried to temper the Most High's wrath against the rebels of Israel, but at least he knew that the only way to resolve the issue was through YAHUAH Himself, and not a man or magic formula.

The next thing Moses does is curious, but should be familiar to us all. He warns YAH that if He wipes out Israel now, then the Egyptians will mock. The argument falls short in a few ways. First, YAHUAH had already torn apart the Egyptians' country, and decapitated its leadership. The Egyptian people were in no position to mock anything. Indeed, Egypt would never again rise as the great power it had been before the Exodus. YAHUAH eliminated their might forever.

But even more than that, the Egyptians were heathens who worshiped false gods. Moses sought to use their supposed opinion as a shield against YAH's opinion. Instead of worrying about what the Egyptians might say about the Most High's ability or intentions, Moses should have been worrying about what YAHUAH had just said about Israel.

The great prophet then urges YAHUAH to remember His covenants with Abraham, Isaac and Jacob in turning away from His fierce wrath.

In all of this, Moses offered one of the most powerful prayers in all of Scripture. But it ignored a few things we should be mindful about. First, YAHUAH can deal with His own reputation if we obey Him. Here,

Moses thought he knew better than YAH with respect to what people would say about the Most High.

Second, had YAHUAH executed His plan to re-start Israel through Moses, ELOHIYM would have still been "***remember[ing] Abraham, Isaac, and Israel, His servants.***" Why? Because Moses was the son of Amram, who was the son of Kohath, who was the son of Levi, who was the son of Jacob, who was the son of Isaac, who was the son of Abraham. In other words, with Moses as the second progenitor of the house of Israel, Moses remained in the line of promise, and YAHUAH would have honored his promises to Abraham, Isaac and Jacob.

So why did Moses fight against the Most High on behalf of the people? He loved and cherished them. He also loved Aaron, Miriam, and Joshua. He likely suspected Aaron's culpability, and wondered whether the Most High would cut off Aaron, or his other family and friends in the judgment.

Moreover, it's also possible that Moses felt he had too much at stake. He might have viewed himself as having put his own reputation on the line as Israel's deliverer. While he was concerned with the Most High's renown, he also may have been a little concerned with his own.

By this time, the prophet might have been too emotionally invested in the thought that he himself had delivered them. He simply could not just give them back to YAHUAH to be consumed in His wrath.

In essence, Moses resisted the Most High's will, directly contradicting the request to 'leave Him alone.' YAHUAH had demanded that Moses offer up the children of promise because of their disobedience. Moses refused.

Despite this disobedience, YAHUAH honored Moses' request. But consider what we saw in the last chapter, where the Most High had demanded that Abraham give up his child of promise.

Offering Up the Children of Promise

Both Abraham and Moses were essentially posed the same question. YAH gave them the same test, although they looked different to Moses in real time. Consider the two men's responses to YAHUAH in these tests.

YAHUAH commanded Abraham to offer up his child of promise, a child who had done nothing wrong. In reply, Abraham immediately obeyed, departing to the mountain to which the Most High directed him, and offering up Isaac as a sacrifice to YAHUAH. The patriarch did not argue with YAH, but simply obeyed. And he did so immediately.

By contrast, Moses did not obey YAH's command, despite the fact that the children of Israel, unlike Isaac, were not innocent. Indeed, the people were exactly as YAHUAH described them: stiffnecked and evil idolaters who deserved the death sentence. Despite their guilt, Moses refused.

Moses could not see how YAHUAH could fulfill His promises if He were to destroy the people. He could not understand the Father's theological calculus, so to speak, so he rejected ABBA's demand to 'offer up' the people. In other words, Moses wrongfully shielded a fugitive people.

Abraham thought differently than Moses. The father of the faith obeyed, and his obedience left room for the Most High to surprise him with grace. ELOHIYM gave a substitute offering, and permitted Abraham to keep his promised child. Why? Because Abraham had passed the test and proved, once and for all, that he loved YAHUAH "***more than these.***"

Moses was offered the same test, the opportunity to offer the children of promise (namely, the whole House of Israel) back to YAHUAH as a sacrifice. But despite the fact that Moses knew that this was the will of the Most High, the prophet rejected His will. Instead, Moses insisted that his own will should take precedence over the Father's will. Abraham had passed the test; Moses failed the test.

And this is the reason why Moses fell in the wilderness nearly forty years later. The people wore him out. These was the same nation he had defended decades earlier, in Exodus 32. Had he let YAHUAH do what He said He wanted to do, Moses would not have been in a position to be striving with ungodly and ungrateful rebels throughout their years in the wilderness.

We should consider one final point here: Abraham obeyed YAHUAH and received his child of promise back to him. He was rewarded by becoming the father of the chosen people. Moses, however, refused to obey YAHUAH's voice, and wrestled out of the Father a reprieve from His judgment. This reprieve, however, was only temporary. Moses himself almost immediately killed three thousand of the offending Israelites, and spent decades fighting the survivors all throughout the wilderness.

In the end, not only did all of the adult men die in the wilderness despite Moses' intercession, but the prophet even lost his own life before he could enter the promised land. Moses' disobedience carried a very high price.

When we refuse to agree with the Most High's judgment, we forfeit our inheritance. We lose the honor the Father prepared for those who obey His voice.

This rejection of YAHUAH's expressed will haunted Moses for the rest of his life. He wrestled with the people in the wilderness because they were there TO wrestle with him. ABBA had proposed to destroy these evildoers. Instead, Moses begged the Father to spare them. Because he did this in opposition to YAH's will, the people he pleaded for came back as a snare in his life. They seduced him to sin by continually angering him.

And Moses himself saw this, and spoke on it in a slightly different context. Deuteronomy 7:16 tells us the following:

> And thou shalt consume all the people which YAHUAH thy ELOHIYM shall deliver thee; thine

> eye shall have no pity upon them: neither shalt thou serve their gods; for that will be a snare unto thee.

Just as the people were to consume the wicked all around them, YAHUAH had commanded Moses to permit Him to consume the wicked of Israel. Just as ABBA warned, the Israelites themselves became a snare to Moses. And the prophet sinned through his anger.

By the time Moses struck the rock, instead of speaking to it, his heart had been shattered from the continual warfare he conducted with the sinning Israelites. He once more disobeyed the Father, and the Father judged him for it. ABBA refused him the honor of bringing the people into the promised land.

The root of Moses' sin at the waters of Meribah did not begin that fateful day, but could be found forty years earlier, in Moses' own disobedience to the Father's command.

Faithful In All the Father's House

A final note is in order here: Moses remains one of the greatest prophets, and one of the greatest men, to ever walk the planet. He was a friend of YAHUAH, and his example in many respects should be followed. As YAHUAH Himself testified in Psalm 103:7, "***He made known his ways unto Moses, his acts unto the children of Israel.***" Moses saw things no one else could see, because he was closer to the Father than anyone else.

Paul testified of Moses, in Hebrews 3:5, "***And Moses verily was faithful in all his house, as a servant,***

for a testimony of those things which were to be spoken after."

Moses remains a towering figure of Scripture. This book by no means urges anyone to think anything to the contrary. The point of this chapter is that, as great as Moses was, he failed YAHUAH's test to love the Most High more than he loved the people to whom the Most High sent him.

Had I been put in the same situation, I have no doubt that I, too, might have fallen as Moses did. May YAHUAH grant all of us the faithfulness of Moses, and even more!

Chapter 5, David

"And if thou wilt walk before me, as David thy father walked, in integrity of heart, and in uprightness, to do according to all that I have commanded thee, and wilt keep my statutes and my judgments"
-1 Kings 9:4

"Because David did that which was right in the eyes of YAHUAH, and turned not aside from any thing that he commanded him all the days of his life, save only in the matter of Uriah the Hittite."
-1 Kings 15:5

David the king led a life so intoxicated with YAHUAH the Father that words almost fail to tell the story. The man modeled a lifelong love affair with YAH, and established a house forever, just as YAHUAH had sought to do with Moses centuries earlier.

His life has so saturated mine, so ignited my soul, that I wrote *Five Smooth Stones: David, the Man After YAH's Own Heart,* about David.[32] In that work, I examine his life in detail. There is so much more to him than can fill any single volume. Nevertheless, I offered my work as homage to my Father for giving me such a great man for an example.

This chapter will not try to recreate what may be found in that text. In these brief pages, we quickly survey the central question put earlier to Abraham and to Moses:

David, did you love YAHUAH more than the things of the world?

The Mean Streets of Bethlehem

The mean streets of Bethlehem took a lot out of David. By mean streets, of course, we mean his own house, and his own family. David was likely the product of an adulterous relationship. By Torah's principles, he ought to have had no right nor inheritance in Israel, certainly not as a future king.

But the young man's troubles ran far deeper than that. The emotional foundation of love that all boys and girls should grow up with found no place in David's life. As the eighth-born son, David was little more than a cast-a-way, an afterthought, a despised toy who found no solace or companionship in his own family. Instead, they mocked and tormented him his entire childhood, even after he was anointed the future king by the prophet Samuel.

David grew up in a house full of narcissists. He found peace only in the Judean hills as he tended sheep. He honed his music with the livestock and the wild animals. His mother and father's emotional abandonment looked perfectly normal to outsiders looking in. This meant that David had to find his own comfort, and his own soul relationships.

He found that friendship in the Most High YAHUAH as a little boy of twelve. He heard the Father's call, and adopted the Father as HIS Father. David never looked back, and learned to rely upon YAHUAH for everything. He talked to him as if He were his own flesh and blood father.

This is the reason why the future prophet, priest and king developed such intimacy with the Father, because he had no choice. Others could rely upon respectable Israelite society, birth order, their looks, their family position. David had none of those.

He needed YAHUAH for everything. He gave himself to the Master entirely, devouring His Torah, loving His laws, statutes and commandments, and seeking to please Him entirely. After a while, it became easy for David to do this. With the exception of his big sister Zeruiah, none of his family members were ever pleased by anything David did, no matter how well done.

David emerged as the greatest man of his generation, a heart so inflamed with YAHUAH that he became the template of the promised Messiah. The Father sent His Son through the seed of David. All throughout the gospels, and for centuries afterwards, people would call the Messiah "the Son of David."

After YAHUAH's Own Heart

Why did David hold such a lofty position? David rose so high because he humbled himself so low. He accounted himself as nothing. All throughout his life, we see a humility unrivaled by anyone around him. ABBA YAHUAH calls him "***a man after mine own heart.***"[33]

What does this description mean? When YAH calls David a man after His own heart, it meant that David loved YAHUAH first and foremost. The son of Jesse concerned himself with the things that mattered to the Most High. He desperately wanted to please ABBA.

We see David's heart throughout the Psalms and in his life story. In Psalm 42:1-2, David writes,

> 1 As the hart panteth after the water brooks, so panteth my soul after thee, O ELOHIYM.
>
> 2 My soul thirsteth for ELOHIYM, for the living ELOHIYM: when shall I come and appear before ELOHIYM?[34]

David longed for the presence of YAHUAH. The hardships of his life caused him to distrust people. Although he loved deeply and fiercely, he relied upon his Heavenly Father for everything. He learned to love Him "***more than these***," more than all the things and people surrounding him.

Loving Him the Foundation for Self-Encouragement

As Psalm 42 continues, we see that he struggled with depression. But he also continually cast his hope on the Most High. As 1 Samuel 30:6 teaches, "***David encouraged himself in YAHUAH his ELOHIYM.***" David learned that one has to encourage oneself in the Father: you can't just wait for the right circumstances, or people, to come along to encourage you. If you do, you might be waiting a long time!

In perhaps the most well-known line in all of literature, Psalm 23:1, David famously wrote,

"***YAHUAH is my shepherd; I shall not want.***" David did not look for any earthly shepherd. His biological father Jesse should have been his first and most natural shepherd, and he failed David. So, too, did Saul, who portrayed himself as a counterfeit dad to the young giant killer. In fact, virtually everyone in his life failed David in one way or another, including his close friend Jonathan. But in the Most High, David found a shepherd, a teacher, a refuge, and a new father.

David loved YAH "***more than these***," and became a man after YAH's own heart, even as a child. Loving YAHUAH more than the people and things around you pleases the Father, but it also does something else: it gives you a new family, a new hope, and new life.

YAHUAH gave David a vision of His home, the temple. This vision inflamed David for the rest of his life, moving the man to seek to dwell with Him forever. This hunger proved the motivating force for David to build a temple through his son, Solomon.

May all YAH's children find the same hope and refuge in YAHUAH that David found!

So Many More

We have now seen how Abraham, Moses, and David each responded to the call from the Most High asking whether they loved Him "***more than these.***" We could, of course, keep going. Every saint in Scripture addressed this call, from Noah to Joseph, from Sarah to Abigail, from Daniel to Esther, from Mary to Paul. Due to time constraints, we confine our assessment to the three people whose lives we lightly touched. But all the people of Scripture confronted this question. Indeed, everyone, everywhere, of every age, must confront the question of whether they loved YAHUAH "***more than these.***"

It is only when we address the question head on and in the right way that the Father can transform us into His tabernacles. He wants to dwell with us. However, if we are filled with anything except His Spirit and the desire to accomplish His will, we are not fit for His redemption and presence.

Before we close, let's look a little more closely at the Tabernacle itself. While a huge subject, a few features may help us better understand the wonderful hope of our calling in YAHUSHA HA MASHIACH.

Chapter 6, A Few More Tabernacle Things

"My tabernacle also shall be with them: yea, I will be their ELOHIYM, and they shall be my people."
-Ezekiel 37:27

"And after that I looked, and behold, the temple of the tabernacle of the testimony in heaven was opened."
-Revelation 15:5

The Tabernacle offers many more lessons for those who strive to love YAHUAH "***more than these***." Every item in the Tabernacle represents a spiritual truth about how to worship the Father properly. We won't exhaust the subject, but we will briefly explore together just a few of the more prominent features of the Tabernacle.

The Freewill Offering Substance

Perhaps one of the first items to note, in Exodus 25, was that the materials for the construction of the Tabernacle came from the people themselves. Neither Moses nor the elders coerced the nation, but requested that they give freewill offerings of the materials, from the gold, silver and brass, to the rams' skins, goats hair, shittim wood and fine linen.

The Father will not receive as an offering that which you are forced to give, or that which costs you nothing. He also won't receive those things that He hasn't prescribed. If, for instance, someone wanted to offer an unclean animal like a pig as an offering, the Father would not accept that, because it is inconsistent with His holy standards.

When we bring offerings to ABBA YAHUAH, we should want to do it. Those of us raising children should instill in our kids, as soon as possible, how important it is to freely give back to the Father that which He has given to us.

Where did all of the stuff that the children of Israel offered even come from, anyway? Weren't they wandering around in the wilderness?

Yes, they were traveling in the wilderness, without access to minerals and precious resources from the land. But remember one key point from Exodus 12:

> 35 And the children of Israel did according to the word of Moses; and they borrowed of the Egyptians jewels of silver, and jewels of gold, and raiment:
>
> 36 And YAHUAH gave the people favour in the sight of the Egyptians, so that they lent unto them such things as they required. And they spoiled the Egyptians.[35]

The children of Israel had labored in Egypt for over a hundred years. During that time, they had received nearly no compensation for their labor. In very specific cases, such as when Pharaoh's daughter hired Jochebed to watch Moses, Israelites might receive wages. However, the children of Israel were mostly unpaid, just as they have been for the majority of their time in the Americas, the Caribbean, and Europe.

When ABBA delivered Israel from Egyptian bondage, He gave them favor in the sight of their slave masters, who willingly gave them reparations. Why? It was repayment for all the unpaid labor they had performed for a century.

In the same way, Genesis 15 promises that the Israelites preparing to leave America, Canada, Brazil and other slave-holding nations will also receive great substance. This is the promised reparations when we leave the lands of our captivity. That passage reads as follows: "***And also that nation, whom they shall serve, will I judge: and afterward shall they come out with great substance.***"[36]

The first time Israel departed from captivity, we went out with great substance. The upcoming departure, which is imminent, will be no different!

But there was a second reason why we received gold, silver, jewelry, and raiment: ABBA knew we needed these materials to build Him a Tabernacle. Think about the spiritual principle here. **YAHUAH ELOHIYM gives His elect great substance to worship freely as He demands. When ELOHIYM truly calls us, He gives tremendous resources for us to use to beautify His name!**

Another principle is also at play. When we offer things to the Father, we cannot offer junk. We can't offer

Him leftovers or trash. He gives us gifts that we can in turn offer back to Him.

Consider this in the context of raising children. Children are the fruit of the womb, a tremendous blessing for those who have been given them. They are not a burden, but a joy. When the Father gave me children, I immediately offered them back to the Father. At the time, I never considered that I was, in my own small way, following in the footsteps of my great-grandfather Abraham, but that is exactly what I was doing! The Ruach led me even before I fully understood the principles at work. He will lead you in the same way when you follow Him.

Just as with Abraham, my Heavenly Father has blessed my children tremendously, more than I could even put into words. It's not a function of my parenting, because I've made many mistakes. But the Father has multiplied my offering, and consecrated them to Himself.

Children raised in the fear and admonition of YAHUAH bring their parents great joy. Many of the problems with children today arise from the fact that most parents never truly and Biblically consecrated and offered their children back to YAHUAH, Who gave them to us.

After the Pattern

Another critical item to keep in mind is that the Father had a pattern for how Israel was to prepare the Tabernacle. They could not "freestyle." They couldn't imitate the temples they had seen in Egypt. They had no right nor authority to make up whatever looked good to them. No, they had to follow the pattern that YAHUAH had delivered to Moses, exactly.

As we seek to live good and fulfilling lives, we have to remind ourselves that it's not for us to freestyle, either. ABBA YAHUAH has a pattern for how He wants us to live. He delivered His Word to us in the holy Scriptures. He also offers Himself freely to us when we pursue Him as David and Moses did. He wants to be our advisor and counselor, but too often, we want what we want, based on what our eyes see.

Paul tells us that we are to walk by faith, and not by sight. Faith in what? Faith in HIM! In Exodus 19:5, Israel was called to obey the Master's voice, not their own. We cannot be holy and consecrated to Him if we are constantly just wanting to live our own way, and do our own thing.

The Father knows what we need infinitely more than we know. We don't even know what the next hour holds for us, let alone the next year or decade. But the One Who designed us knows all of that, and more. Why shouldn't we be spending as much time as possible in prayer, seeking His guidance?

Is Facebook, Instagram, YouTube, Discord, Twitter, and Snapchat really so much better than hearing from the ELOHIYM Who created and knows everything?

The Ark of the Covenant

ABBA wanted Israel to make an ark out of shittim wood, also known as acacia wood. This is the exact same wood used to prepare Noah's ark. It kept Noah and his family safe for months while being battered by the stormiest and choppiest waters ever to surge over the planet.

What was to go inside the ark? The Ten Commandments, engraved on sapphire stone tablets. This was the heart of the marital covenant between YAHUAH and Israel. It was as if the wedding vows and the wedding program were hidden away in a special chest as a keepsake.

This was important, because Israel's power derived solely from the nation's connection with the Father. When they went against their enemies in battle, they would prevail only to the degree that they were walking in holiness and in conformity to His statutes and commandments.

The Gold of the Tabernacle

Many of the items in the Tabernacle, from the altar of burnt offerings, to the menorah candlesticks, to the utensils, spoons, forks, cups, bowls, and others, were made of pure gold, or covered in gold. This was for two reasons. First, as we saw earlier, the furniture and features of the earthly Tabernacle were designed after the original in Heaven. Fidelity to what YAHUAH has done in Heaven is required for the Father to dwell with us.

The second reason is equally important. Gold signifies royalty. The Tabernacle of Moses, and the Temple of Solomon, each housed the Holy One of Israel. The One Who dwelt in both the Tabernacle, and later the

Temple, was the King of kings. To worship Him, the House of Israel and those who are grafted in must recognize His royal personage. As Malachi tells us, He is a great King Who must be obeyed in all things.

The Altar of Incense

The altar of incense, described in Exodus 30, represented something very special in the life of the children of Israel. Incense, the burning of a sweet aroma, constitutes an important part not only in Israelite worship, but in many religious traditions. But for the true worship of YAHUAH, it not only stands for the offer of sweet aromas to our King. Instead, it symbolizes the prayers of the saints. We know this because Revelation 8 shows us:

> 3 And another angel came and stood at the altar, having a golden censer; and there was given unto him much incense, that he should offer it with the prayers of all saints upon the golden altar which was before the throne.
>
> 4 And the smoke of the incense, which came with the prayers of the saints, ascended up before YAHUAH out of the angel's hand.[37]

The smoke of the incense in heaven ascended up "***with the prayers of the saints.***" The Father loves the prayers of His people. 1 Thessalonians 5:17 commands YAH's children to "***pray without ceasing.***"

Just as heaven featured a golden altar of incense, so, too, did the Tabernacle of Moses feature a golden altar. Although carved of the same shittim wood as the ark, it was to be covered in pure gold.

The Colors of the Clothing and the Curtains

Gold, blue, purple and scarlet filled many of the cloth items associated with the Tabernacle, from the curtains to the priests' clothing. These colors all relate to features of the Most High's order. As we saw above, gold is the color of royalty. Blue is the color of holiness. Purple is worn by kings. And scarlet relates to the blood of the sacrifices required to propitiate YAHUAH. The scarlet color, along with all of the sacrifices, point to the final blood sacrifice of our true Passover Lamb, Adonai YAHUSHA HA MASHIACH.

Linen in the Tabernacle

The curtains and hangings of the Tabernacle consisted of "fine twined linen." So, too, did the priests' garments, pants, and robes. Linen is a holy, high frequency fabric. It vibrates at 5,000 Hz, the highest frequency of any fabric except wool, which also vibrates at 5,000 Hz.

The fabrics of the Tabernacle needed to vibrate at such a high energy level because the Tabernacle was a holy and sanctified place. YAHUAH Himself met with the people there, after all.

Linen was also chosen because the angels and the saints of Heaven also wear linen robes. Revelation 15:6 describes the seven angels of judgment as follows: "***And the seven angels came out of the temple, having the seven plagues, clothed in pure and white linen, and having their breasts girded with golden girdles.***"

In a similar way, the saints who follow the Lamb also wear linen:

> 7 Let us be glad and rejoice, and give honour to him: for the marriage of the Lamb is come, and his wife hath made herself ready.
>
> 8 And to her was granted that she should be arrayed in fine linen, clean and white: for the fine linen is the righteousness of saints.[38]

The wearing of linen, as Revelation 19 tells us, is a gift, something granted to us. Why? Because the linen represents righteousness, both the righteousness of the saints as well as the righteousness of YAHUSHA HA MASHIACH, YAH's sacrificial Lamb. Those who are redeemed, who follow the Lamb wherever He goes and who love Him "***more than these***," must be clothed in His righteousness.

The Burnt Offering

We will explore one final item which forms part of the Tabernacle worship system. This item differs slightly from the others because it actually predates YAHUAH's command to Moses to build the Tabernacle.

All deities demand worship and sacrifices. YAHUAH also demands a sacrifice. Sacrifices are designed to appease, or propitiate, the displeasure of the one to whom the sacrifice is offered.

In total, the Father demanded five different forms of offerings from the children of Israel: the sin offering, the meal offering, the wave offering, the trespass offering, the peace offering, and the burnt offering.

The foundation of the sacrificial system instituted by the Father was the burnt offering. It is mentioned about two hundred and sixty times in the Bible, not including the apocryphal books such as Enoch, 1 and 2 Esdras and the Maccabees.

The first burnt offering we see is in Genesis 8, when Noah emerged from the Flood, and offered a burnt offering of every clean animal. Next, in Genesis 22, YAHUAH directs Abraham to offer up his beloved son as a burnt offering on Mount Moriah.

In the burnt offering, the worshipers offered the unblemished male animal as a sacrifice to YAHUAH by fire. It constituted a sweet incense to the fire. Why? Because it showed the entirety of the sacrifice was given to the Father. It was all burned in fire.

When Solomon built the Temple five centuries later, his burnt offerings were consumed by fire coming down from YAHUAH in Heaven.

The truly exceptional aspect of the burnt offering is that it prefigured Messiah YAHUSHA's sacrifice in a very special way. By His sinless life and sacrificial death, He fulfilled all five of the offerings of the worship system. However, the burnt offering demonstrated YAHUSHA's perfect work in the purest way possible.

What did Messiah do? He offered everything in His life to the Father. He held nothing back, and loved YAHUAH with a perfect love.

When we follow the Lamb, we are spiritually joined to Him. We offer ourselves up as burnt offerings to the Father through the Son. Paul discussed this phenomenon in Romans 12:1-2:

> 1 I beseech you therefore, brethren, by the mercies of YAHUAH, that ye present your bodies a living sacrifice, holy, acceptable unto YAHUAH, which is your reasonable service.
>
> 2 And be not conformed to this world: but be ye transformed by the renewing of your mind, that ye may prove what is that good, and acceptable, and perfect, will of ELOHIYM.

The saints who follow the Lamb, who are to become the Tabernacle of the Most High, must present themselves to the Father as a living sacrifice. We must be consumed with His will, more than our own desires, or the desires of anyone else.

Also, we must intentionally and continuously present ourselves to YAHUAH. Consecration to the Father does not happen by accident. It takes serious and intense prayer, and meditation on His Word. We have to study what He says to us, and work both Scripture and His specific directions to us into our thinking. We can't be casual about it.

The burnt offering was consumed by fire. Fire laps up everything it touches, and destroys it. In the same way, we know that YAHUAH is fire, as He tells us in Deuteronomy 4:24 and Hebrews 12:29. Since He is fire, we must be engulfed in what He desires for us, laying our own desires aside. This is what YAHUSHA meant in the Garden of Gethsemane when He said, "***nevertheless, not my will, but thine, be done.***"[39]

When we give ourselves to the will of the Father, we are consumed by Him, and become what He wants us to be. We become like the angel of YAHUAH who appeared to Moses in the burning bush in Exodus 3. We remain distinct, individual human beings, but become people who merge into the Father's will. We become living extensions of Him, and only in His fire will we be free to be what He intended us to be. And our joy comes from doing His will, even when it hurts.

§ § §

The Tabernacle offers many, many more treasures that a thorough study could explore. The goal of this book on the subject, like many of the topics treated here, is not to be exhaustive, but illustrative. These pages offer considerations for you to take back to the Father in your times of meditation, study, and prayer.

May ABBA unlock to you many more secrets of His kingdom!

Chapter 7, Why This All Matters Now

Many of the things in this book are things that you will have read before, or previously heard from your pastor or Bible teacher. But this era in which we live resembles no other time in history, except one.

The Days of Noah

In Luke 17:26, YAHUSHA teaches, "***And as it was in the days of Noe, so shall it be also in the days of the Son of man.***" YAHUSHA, the Son of Man, is very near to return for judgment in His Second Coming. The days we have entered are the days of Noah. In other words, what life looked like in Noah's time is what life now looks like in our time.

We have reached a season of prophecy, a season foretold by Mashiach in Matthew 24 and Luke 21, and also in the Book of Daniel, and in the Revelation. The time to play games with YAHUAH has come to an end. Now is the time when He has begun to cut off the wicked. Suddenly.

Did you know that the wicked are not merely those who offer blood sacrifices to demons, or worship false gods? No, Beloved, the wicked are those who fail to conform their lives to the Father's statutes. The wicked are the people who do not have YAHUAH's laws and commandments in their hearts. This is why Revelation 14:12 warns that the saints are those who keep the commandments of YAHUAH, and guard the faith of YAHUSHA.

In other words, the saints follow the Lamb whithersoever He goes. The saints live with YAHUAH. The saints love and adore YAHUAH.

Do You Love YAHUAH More Than These?

The most important question for those who follow the Lamb wherever He goes is this: do you love YAHUAH ***more than these***? Do you love YAHUAH more than your family and your money, your friends and your job, your status in society and the things you possess?

The Father will not forgive those who love anything more than Him. He will not pardon those who keep anything in their lives back for themselves. Have you sacrificed ***your*** Isaac, the Father's promise to you, on the altar of YAHUAH's desires? Or have you selfishly kept your Isaac for yourself?

Have you thought, like Moses, that you knew better than the Most High concerning how to handle the gifts He gave you? If ABBA gives you anything, you are expected to offer it back to Him. But do you trust Him enough to do it?

Before I became a true believer, I thought I already was one, because I went to church. But I didn't know that going to church doesn't make you a believer any more than standing in a garage makes you a car. I thought I was on the path of righteousness by virtue of where my parents had taken me on Sunday mornings.

I had no clue that YAHUAH hates the self-righteous, and despises those who live only for themselves, and depart from His commandments. He hates those who refuse to give Him EVERYTHING!

Giving Him Everything

Today is the day for us to give everything back to the Father. It all came from Him anyway. Where did we get our money, or our skills, abilities, or energy? Didn't the Most High El of Israel give us everything? We need to start living like He did!

The only way to become YAHUAH's Tabernacle, and to receive everlasting life, is to love YAH more than anything else. Our eternal destiny depends on it.

Now, in light of everything you have read, what are you going to do? Heaven is watching. The Most High is waiting. It's time to follow the Lamb wherever He goes. It's time to walk in the narrow way.

Satan is looking at that tiny remnant who have decided to offer up everything to YAHUAH. The devil glares at us with fury. He hears Messiah's voice in his ears, rolling through his chest. A single word thunders throughout his being: Checkmate.

The living tabernacles of YAHUAH, you and me, are the very judgment of the devil and his angels. That's why Paul asks in 1 Corinthians 6:3, "***Know ye not that we shall judge angels?***" What angels is Paul talking about? The devil and his angels!

By walking in the Most High's power, we allow His will for us to dominate every decision we make and preference we exercise. We allow His power to flow through our lives. We literally allow ELOHIYM to say of us in Jeremiah 51:20:

> 20 Thou art my battle axe and weapons of war: for with thee will I break in pieces the nations, and with thee will I destroy kingdoms;

Beloved, Satan looks at you and me with anguish and rage, because he recognizes his judges when he sees us. He recognizes that, in the Most High's hands, you and I are His Tabernacle, His battle axe, and His weapons of war.

When you submit everything to YAHUAH, you literally ***become*** the victory in YAHUSHA HA MASHIACH.

May YAHUAH ELOHIYM usher you into all truth. So be it! Shalom!

Acknowledgments

Once more, I stand in gratitude and reverence at the goodness of ABBA YAHUAH to permit me to share some of His testimony.

Heavenly Father, I thank and praise You for the newness of life You have given me, and the power of Your Word. May You multiply the reach of these pages a thousandfold for Your honor alone. May You be glorified, praised, and adored forever. To You alone YAHUAH ELOHIYM, and Your Son YAHUSHA HA MASHIACH, and to You, Ruach ha Qodesh, be glory and honor in the set-apart assemblies!

I also owe thanks to my family, my true family. You have been my beloved. Throughout this writing, you have nurtured and cared for me, encouraged and strengthened me, and I acknowledge you with eternal gratitude. You have listened to these concepts in many Sabbath lessons, commutes, and dinner conversations. You have endured my sometimes maniacal focus as I tried to understand the revelations of Scripture. Sometimes, my thoughts are of my own origin. Sometimes, the Father has been pleased to share new things with me. But in all, you have been with me. I love you and thank you for being you, and for submitting yourselves to Him.

To the new friends I have been winning in the journey, may ABBA perfect your wisdom and understanding in the knowledge of Him. I thank my

Father for bringing each of you into my life. You know who you are. You have touched me in countless ways, and I pray that these words strengthen you through your own challenges and trials.

I have also been saddened to learn that the people you start out with are not always those with whom you finish. Many of the people with whom I thought I would fight on the battlefield side-by-side are no longer to be found, or no longer interested in a man who does not lay his life down to be plundered, exploited, and used. But even to you, I owe a debt of gratitude. You have taught me to hew even more closely to the Father. You have helped me to abandon my own often faulty sense of who people are, and to rely instead only upon the wisdom and direction of my Father. Sometimes, it's a painful wisdom. But it's always a RIGHT wisdom. So, thank you, friends of the past, critics, slanderers, former bosses, and those who have cursed me out in public and in private. I am a better soul today because of the wounds I have suffered at your hands.

And once again, to the dear readers who have borne with me through yet another adventure through Scripture, thank you! May ABBA increase your wisdom, give you His heart, and magnify Himself in your life yet more and more.

Now to YAHUAH only wise be glory and majesty, dominion and power, both now and forever. So be it! HalleluYAH!!!

End Notes

[1] Exodus 19:4-6.

[2] Exodus 19:8.

[3] David Israel, *Five Smooth Stones: David, the Man After YAH's Own Heart*, Decatur: The Key of David Press, 2022, pp. 289-290.

[4] 1 Chronicles 22:19

[5] Psalm 29:1.

[6] Revelation 21:3.

[7] Luke 17:21.

[8] John 21:15 reads, "So when they had dined, YAHUSHA saith to Simon Peter, Simon, son of Jonas, lovest thou me more than these? He saith unto him, Yea, Adonai; thou knowest that I love thee. He saith unto him, Feed my lambs."

[9] Matthew 10:37-39.

[10] Matthew 7:13-14.

[11] Matthew 12:48-50.

[12] Mark 10:17-22.

[13] Revelation 14:1-4.

[14] Ezekiel 9:4.

[15] Exodus 33:15.

[16] James 1:27.

[17] Revelation 14:4.

[18] Genesis 12:1-3.

[19] Genesis 12:1-4.

[20] Genesis 13:13.

[21] Genesis 13:10-12.

[22] Genesis 18:20-21.

[23] Genesis 13:14.

[24] Genesis 22:1-2.

[25] Genesis 22:3.

[26] Genesis 22:8.

[27] Genesis 22:10.

[28] Genesis 22:12.

[29] Psalm 106:32-33.

[30] Exodus 32:9-10.

[31] Exodus 32:11-13.

[32] David Israel, *Five Smooth Stones.*

[33] 1 Samuel 13:14.

---

[34] Psalm 42:1-2.
[35] Exodus 12:35-36.
[36] Genesis 15:14.
[37] Revelation 8:3-4.
[38] Revelation 19:7-8.
[39] Luke 22:42.

ɔduct-compliance